LINE GRAPHS

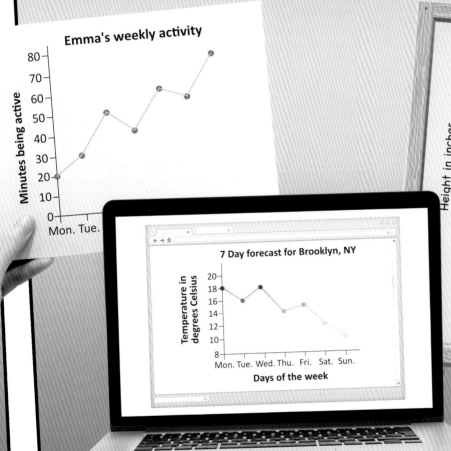

Emma's weekly activity

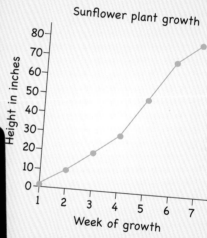

Sunflower plant growth

7 Day forecast for Brooklyn, NY

Lizann Flatt

Crabtree Publishing Company

www.crabtreebooks.com

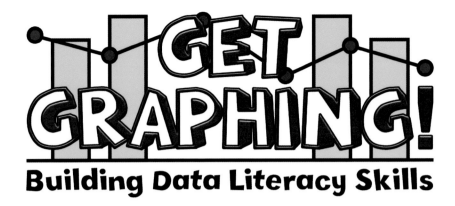

GET GRAPHING!
Building Data Literacy Skills

Author: Lizann Flatt

Series research and development:
Reagan Miller

Editorial director: Kathy Middleton

Substantive editor: Crystal Sikkens

Proofreader: Janine Deschenes

Indexer: Petrice Custance

Photo research: Crystal Sikkens,
Katherine Berti

Design: Katherine Berti

Print and production coordinator:
Katherine Berti

Image credits:
All images by Shutterstock

Library and Archives Canada Cataloguing in Publication

Flatt, Lizann, author
     Line graphs / Lizann Flatt.

(Get graphing! Building data literacy skills)
Includes index.
Issued in print and electronic formats.
ISBN 978-0-7787-2625-8 (hardback).--
ISBN 978-0-7787-2635-7 (paperback).--
ISBN 978-1-4271-1838-7 (html)

     1. Graphic methods--Juvenile literature. 2. Charts, diagrams, etc.--
Juvenile literature. 3. Mathematics--Charts, diagrams, etc.--Juvenile
literature. I. Title.

QA90.F53 2016   j518'.23   C2016-903317-1
                                        C2016-903318-X

Library of Congress Cataloging-in-Publication Data

CIP available at the Library of Congress

Crabtree Publishing Company
www.crabtreebooks.com   1-800-387-7650

Printed in Canada/072016/EF20160630

Published in Canada
Crabtree Publishing
616 Welland Ave.
St. Catharines, Ontario
L2M 5V6

Published in the United States
Crabtree Publishing
PMB 59051
350 Fifth Avenue, 59th Floor
New York, New York 10118

Published in the United Kingdom
Crabtree Publishing
Maritime House
Basin Road North, Hove
BN41 1WR

Published in Australia
Crabtree Publishing
3 Charles Street
Coburg North
VIC 3058

Contents

Questions and Answers

Have you ever had a question you needed or wanted an answer to? Some questions can be answered by finding information in books, newspapers, magazines, or on the Internet. Sometimes you can find answers if you collect your own information.

This boy is collecting information from this weather station.

4

Collecting Data

Data is collected information. It can be collected in many forms, such as measurements of height or temperature, amounts of money or time, or a **tally**. Data can be shared in a type of drawing called a graph. Graphs use lines, colors, and pictures to organize data, making it easier to understand.

My sleep hours

Night of the Week	Hours Slept
Monday	11
Tuesday	10
Wednesday	10
Thursday	8
Friday	7
Saturday	10
Sunday	11

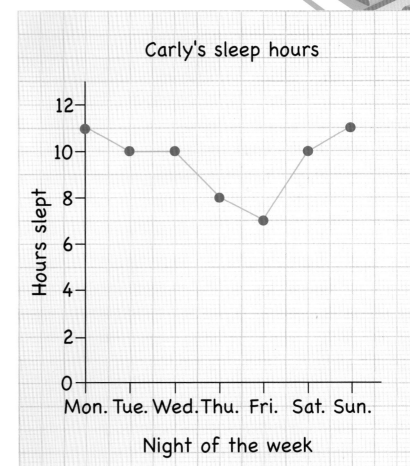

Carly's sleep hours

Carly recorded how much sleep she got each night for a week on this table.

Carly then used the data recorded on the table to create this graph.

5

Great Graphs

A graph shows information so that other people can understand it quickly and easily. There are many different kinds of graphs. Bar graphs, picture graphs, and line graphs are some of the most common kinds of graphs. Each kind of graph shows a different type of information.

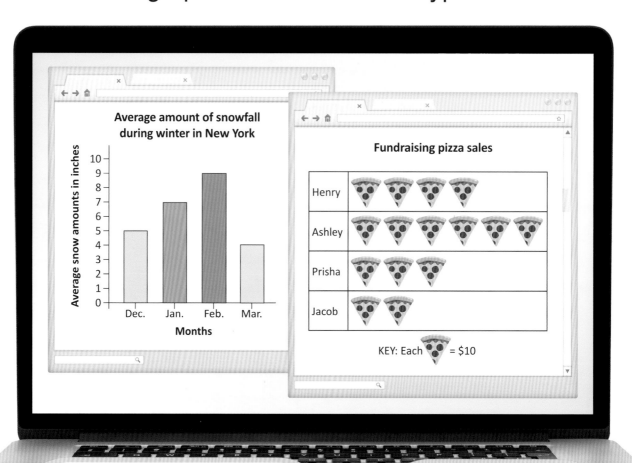

*A bar graph uses colored bars to **compare** data or show larger changes over time.*

A picture graph uses pictures to compare information.

Line Graphs

In this book, you will learn about line graphs. Line graphs show data changes over time just like a bar graph, but instead of bars it uses points and lines to show information.

Parts of a Line Graph

All line graphs have the same basic parts. Each part has an important purpose. Once you know the parts and their purpose, you will be able to correctly read and create your own line graphs.

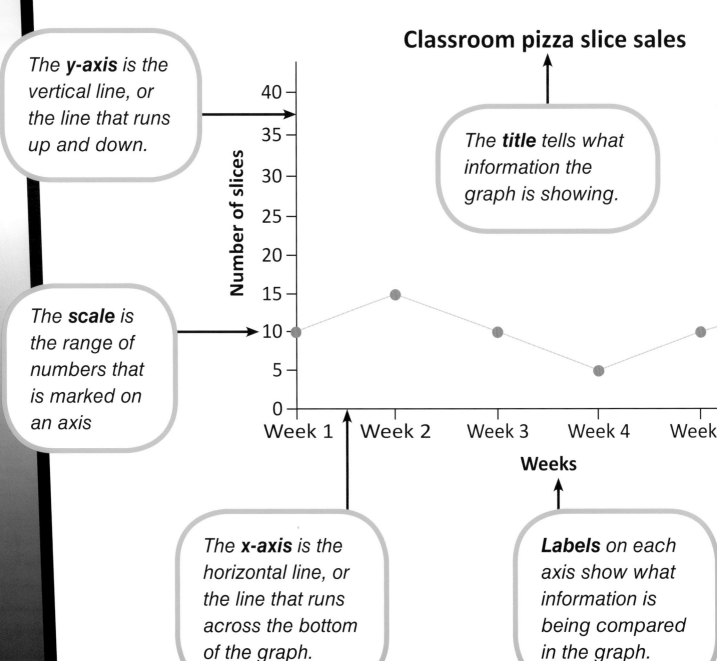

The **y-axis** is the vertical line, or the line that runs up and down.

Classroom pizza slice sales

The **title** tells what information the graph is showing.

The **scale** is the range of numbers that is marked on an axis

The **x-axis** is the horizontal line, or the line that runs across the bottom of the graph.

Labels on each axis show what information is being compared in the graph.

Be a Data Detective!

How do the points and lines of a line graph work together?

Points show the data.

Lines connect each point in order from left to right.

Week 6   Week 7   Week 8

The **categories** show what each point represents.

A Look at Lines

The lines on a bar graph help to give a quick look at the **results** of the data collected. If the line on a graph is going up, it means there was an increase in the data measured. A line that is going down means there was a decrease in the data. A line that is straight across means there was little or no change.

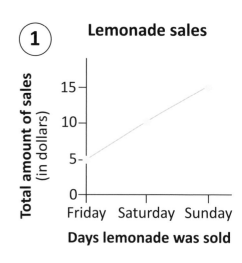

1

Lemonade sales

Total amount of sales (in dollars)

Friday Saturday Sunday

Days lemonade was sold

2

Lemonade sales

Total amount of sales (in dollars)

Friday Saturday Sunday

Days lemonade was sold

Be a Data Detective!

Look at these three graphs. Which one shows a decrease in sales? How do you know?

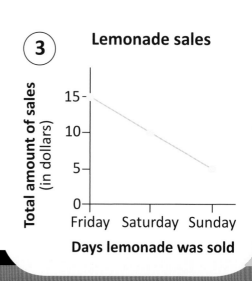

3

Lemonade sales

Total amount of sales (in dollars)

Friday Saturday Sunday

Days lemonade was sold

Data Changes

To tell if the change between data points is large or small, you can look at how **steep** the lines going up or down are. It can also tell you how quickly the data changed.

Be a Data Detective!

Which of the two graphs below show a greater change in data? How do you know?

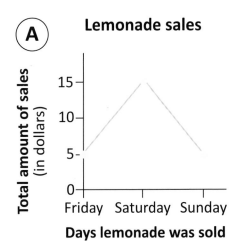

(A) **Lemonade sales**

Total amount of sales (in dollars)

15
10
5
0

Friday Saturday Sunday

Days lemonade was sold

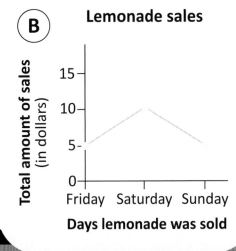

(B) **Lemonade sales**

Total amount of sales (in dollars)

15
10
5
0

Friday Saturday Sunday

Days lemonade was sold

Predicting and Patterns

The lines on a line graph can also help to **predict** future data. If a line is going up, it may continue to go up in the future. If a line is going down, it may continue to go down. If the line stays flat it may continue that way. The general direction the data is moving in is sometimes called a **trend**. A line graph makes trends easier to see.

Even if the lines go up and down between points, a graph can still show an upward trend as long as the overall direction of the lines is moving upward.

DAILY NEWS

World - Business - Finance - Lifestyle - Travel - Sport - Weather

Issue: 240104   THE WORLDS BEST SELLING NATIONAL NEWSPAPER   Est - 1965

First Edition   Monday 5th June

Seven day forecast for Brooklyn, NY

Temperature in degrees Celsius

20 – 18 – 16 – 14 – 12 – 10 – 8

Mon. Tue. Wed. Thu. Fri. Sat. Sun.

Days of the week

Patterns

Looking for **patterns** in a line graph can also help to predict data in the future. If a line graph showed a flat line, then an upward line, and then a flat line and an upward line again, it is possible the future data will show this same pattern.

Be a Data Detective!

Based on the pattern in the graph below, do you think the temperature for Wednesday overnight will go up or down?

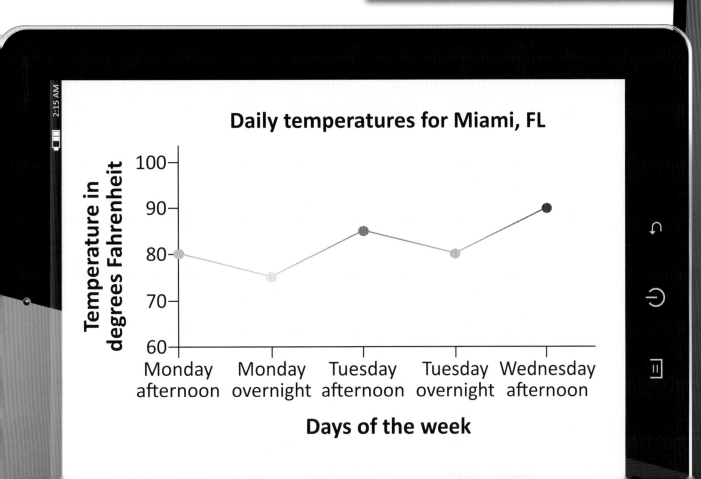

Daily temperatures for Miami, FL

Temperature in degrees Fahrenheit

100 —
90 —
80 —
70 —
60 —

Monday afternoon — Monday overnight — Tuesday afternoon — Tuesday overnight — Wednesday afternoon

Days of the week

2:15 AM

Gathering Data

Jackson West is in Grade 2. His teacher, Ms. Wilson, told the class that for the next month they will be tracking their healthy habits. Each student is going to keep a record of their own data. They will begin by keeping track of how much water they drink each day for a week.

Tracking your healthy habits

Recording Data

Jackson decides to record his data on a **tally chart**. He will add one **tally mark** to his chart every time he drinks a glass of water. Whenever he drinks from the water fountain at school, he will also count that as a glass of water.

Jackson's glasses of water

Day of the week	Glasses of water
Monday	|
Tuesday	||
Wednesday	||
Thursday	|||
Friday	卌
Saturday	卌 ||
Sunday	卌 |||

Get Graphing

Now that Jackson has his data, he creates a line graph to share his information with the rest of the class. He begins by drawing the y-axis and labels it "Glasses of water." He then draws and labels the x-axis "Days of the week." He evenly spaces the days along the x-axis.

Jackson's glasses of water

Glasses of water

Days of the week

Time periods such as the days of the week, years, or months go along the x-axis of a line graph.

Set the Scale

Now, Jackson needs to decide the scale for the y-axis. A scale shows all of the data points and makes them easy to read. The lowest number in Jackson's tally chart was 1 and the highest was 8. He gives each number its own line since they could fit easily on his paper. He begins his scale at 0, where the y-axis and x-axis meet.

The scale should evenly space the data on the y-axis with enough room to show the data clearly.

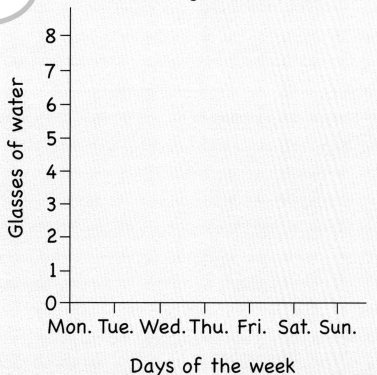

Jackson's glasses of water

Place the Points

Jackson can now add his data to the line graph. He uses his tally chart to find the data for Monday. Then, on his line graph, he finds the mark on the x-axis for Monday and moves his pencil up until it is in line with the 1 on the y-axis. He makes a point there. He continues adding points to the graph using the data from the rest of the week. After he's finished, he connects the points with lines.

Jackson's glasses of water

Day of the week	Glasses of water
Monday	|
Tuesday	||
Wednesday	||
Thursday	|||
Friday	ⴄ
Saturday	ⴄ ||
Sunday	ⴄ |||

Be a Data Detective!

Answer the below questions using Jackson's graph.

1. Which day did Jackson drink the most water?

2. How many more glasses did Jackson drink on Sunday than on Monday?

Jackson made the points a different color than the lines to help the data stand out.

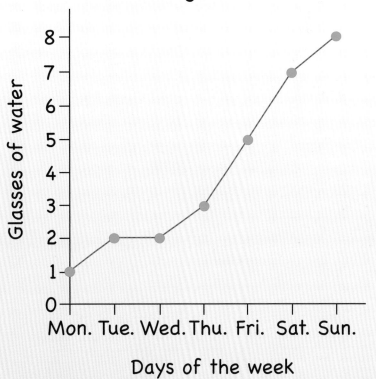

Jackson's glasses of water

Glasses of water — Days of the week

Being Active

After the class had collected and graphed the amount of water they drank, Ms. Wilson said the next step of tracking their health was to find out how active they were. Each person needed to keep track of the total number of minutes a day they spent being active, such as walking, running, skipping, playing sports, etc.

Jackson recorded his results in the table below.

Days of the week	Number of minutes being active			Total
Monday	15 min Played soccer during morning recess	15 min Played tag during afternoon recess recess	30 min Bike ride with mom	60 min
Tuesday	10 min Jumped rope before school	30 min Swimming class		40 min
Wednesday	30 min Played basketball during gym class	50 min Took my dog to the park		80 min
Thursday	10 min Rode my bike to school	10 min Rode my bike home from school	10 min Walked to my grandparent's house	30 min
Friday	20 min Played on jungle gym before school	10 min Rode my bike to my friend's house		30 min
Saturday	20 min Walked my dog	30 min Swimming class		50 min
Sunday	20 min Played hopscotch in my driveway			20 min

Now it's Your Turn!

Using the total minutes in Jackson's table, create a line graph to show how active Jackson was over the week. You can use the checklist to help you.

Checklist of items for your graph:

✔ *title*
✔ *x-axis label*
✔ *y-axis label*
✔ *scale*
✔ *points*
✔ *lines*
✔ *categories*

Emma's Results

Be a Data Detective!

Jackson's friend Emma also tracked how active she was over the week. Her results are in the table on the right.

1. Which line graph below correctly shows the results on Emma's table?

2. Do you see a trend in either graph?

Emma's active table

Day of the week	Minutes being active
Monday	20 min.
Tuesday	30 min.
Wednesday	50 min.
Thursday	40 min.
Friday	60 min.
Saturday	55 min.
Sunday	75 min.

(A)
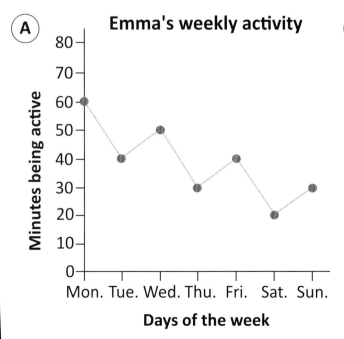

(B)
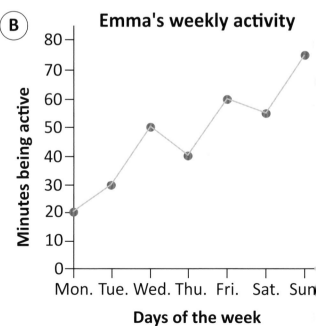

Learning More

Books

Piddock, *Claire. Line, Bar, and Circle Graphs* (My Path to Math). Crabtree Publishing Company, 2010.

Shea, Mary Molly. *Making Line Graphs* (Graph It!). Gareth Stevens Publishing, 2015.

Cocca, Lisa Colozza. *Line Graphs* (Making and Using Graphs). Cherry Lake Publishing, 2013.

Websites

This website includes a video along with fun games, activities, and quizzes all about tally charts and line graphs.
https://jr.brainpop.com/math/data/linegraphs/preview.weml

Take a quiz to see how well you understand line graphs.
https://ca.ixl.com/math/grade-2/interpret-line-graphs

Use the given data to find out which line graph is correct at:
https://ca.ixl.com/math/grade-2/which-line-graph-is-correct

About the Author

Lizann Flatt has written many nonfiction books for children. You can find her online at www.lizannflatt.com

Get Graphing Online!

You can also create graphs online! The link below has a list of websites that let you type in your data to create your own graphs. Most of these websites let you print or save your graph when you are finished. You can begin by making different bar graphs using the data found in this book.

http://interactivesites. weebly.com/graphing.html

Glossary

Note: Some boldfaced words are defined where they appear in the text.

compare To find out how things are similar or different

data Information that is gathered or collected

pattern Data that follows a certain rule or order

predict To estimate that something will happen in the future

results An outcome or answers obtained through research

steep Describing a line that rises or falls very sharply or quickly, which looks almost straight up or down

tally A counted amount

tally chart A way to show data using tally marks in a table

tally mark A vertical or diagonal line used for counting

trend The general direction in which something is changing or moving

Index

Answers

Page 9: The points show the data and the lines connect the points.

Page 10: 3—The line is going down.

Page 11: A—There is a steeper line going up.

Page 13: Down

Page 19: 1. Sunday
2. 7

Page 22: 1. B
2. A shows a downward trend, B shows an upward trend.